MARIAN PRAYERS

PRAYERS & DEVOTIONS TO THE BLESSED VIRGIN MARY

All booklets are published thanks to the generosity of the supporters of the Catholic Truth Society

CATHOLIC TRUTH SOCIETY — PUBLISHERS TO THE HOLY SEE

www.ctsbooks.org

All rights reserved. Published 2012 by The Incorporated Catholic Truth Society, 42-46 Harleyford Road, London SE11 5AY. Tel: 020 7640 0042. Compilation and design © 2012 The Incorporated Catholic Truth Society.

Extracts from *The Roman Missal* © 2010, International Commission on English in the Liturgy Corporation.

Latin text of *Missale Romanum*, *Libreria Editrice Vaticana omnia sibi vindicat iura. Sine eiusdem licentia scripto data liceat hunc Missale denuo imprimere aut in aliam linguam vertere.*

Extracts from scripture from the *Jerusalem Bible* © 1966 Darton Longman and Todd and Doubleday & Company inc.

The following prayers are extracted from *The cult of the Virgin Mary in Anglo-Saxon England,* Mary Clayton © Cambridge University Press 1990, reproduced with permission. Page 55: St Aldhelm's Prayer, *In Basilica Beatæ Mariæ semper Virginis (*c. 685). Page 56: St Bede's Prayer, *In natali sanctæ Dei genitricis.* Page 57: The Prayer from the *Book of Nunnaminster* (9th century). Page 59: *Book of Cerne* (9th century); Winchcombe Psalter Prayer (Mid eleventh century). Page 60: Aelfwine Winchester Prayer and the Litany (Written between 1023 and 1035). Page 61: *Oratio ad dei Genitricem.*

ISBN 978 1 86082 797 6

Contents

Introduction 5

Standard Marian prayers 7

Prayers from the Missal and Breviary 15

The Rosary of the Blessed Virgin Mary 39

The Litany of Loreto 47

Prayers from English sources 53

Prayers from approved Marian Apparitions 71

Orthodox Church prayers 79

Other Marian prayers and devotions 83

Marian Hymns 93

Mary in the Bible 107

References 112

INTRODUCTION

The Mother of the Redeemer has a precise place in the plan of salvation, for "when the time had fully come, God sent forth his Son, born of woman, born under the law, to redeem those who were under the law, so that we might receive adoption as sons." (*Ga* 4:4-6)

These words of the Apostle Paul celebrate together the love of the Father, the mission of the Son, the gift of the Spirit, the role of the woman from whom the Redeemer was born, and our own divine filiation. In the Incarnation, the Church encounters Christ and Mary indissolubly joined: he who is the Church's Lord and Head and she who, uttering the first *fiat* of the New Covenant, prefigures the Church's condition as spouse and mother.

Strengthened by the presence of Christ (*Mt* 28:20), the Church journeys through time towards the consummation of the ages and goes to meet the Lord who comes. But on this journey she proceeds along the path already trodden by the Virgin Mary, who "advanced in her pilgrimage of faith, and loyally persevered in her union with her Son unto the cross."

(Adapted from *Redemptoris Mater*, "The Mother of the Redeemer," 1, 2, Pope John Paul II, 1987)

STANDARD MARIAN PRAYERS

Hail Mary

The first line is the Salutation of the Archangel Gabriel to the Blessed Virgin Mary the future mother of Jesus. The second and third lines are the words of Elizabeth, her cousin; the addition of the word 'Jesus' is attributed to Pope Urban IV (1261-64), while the concluding petition reached its present form in 1514.

Ave María, gratia plena, Dóminus tecum; benedícta tu in muliéribus, et benedíctus fructus ventris tui, Iesus.	Hail Mary, full of grace; the Lord is with thee: blessed art thou among women, and blessed is the fruit of thy womb, Jesus.
Sancta Maria, Mater Dei, ora pro nobis peccatoribus, nunc et in hora mortis nostræ. Amen.	Holy Mary, Mother of God, pray for us sinners, now and at the hour of our death. Amen.

Morning Offering Prayer

This Morning Offering prayer is said by many Catholics throughout the world, each morning, to fulfil the request of Our Lady of Fatima for the sanctification of daily duties as a condition for the conversion of all people.

O My God, in union with the Immaculate Heart of Mary
   (here kiss your Brown Scapular),
I offer Thee the Precious Blood of Jesus
   from all the altars throughout the world,
joining with it the offering of my every thought,
   word and action of this day.

O My Jesus, I desire today to gain every indulgence
   and merit I can and I offer them,
together with myself,
to Mary Immaculate that she may best apply them
   to the interests of Thy most Sacred Heart.
Precious Blood of Jesus, save us!
Immaculate Heart of Mary, pray for us!
Sacred Heart of Jesus, Have mercy on us!

Consecration to the Immaculate Heart of Mary

Virgin Mary, Mother of God and our Mother,
to your Immaculate Heart we consecrate ourselves,
in an act of total entrustment to the Lord.
By you we will be led to Christ.
By Him and with Him we will be led to the Father.

We will walk in the light of faith,
and we will do everything so that the world may believe
that Jesus Christ is the One sent by the Father.
With Him we wish to carry His Love and Salvation to the ends of the earth.
Under the protection of your Immaculate Heart,
we will be one People with Christ.
We will be witnesses of His Resurrection.
By Him we will be led to the Father,
for the glory of the Most Holy Trinity,
Whom we adore, praise and bless forever. Amen.

Magnificat

This is Mary's hymn of praise to God in St Luke's Gospel (Lk 1:46-55) on the occasion of her Visitation to St Elizabeth.

Magnificat ánima mea dóminum,	My soul glorifies the Lord, my spirit rejoices in God my saviour.
et exsultávit spíritus meus in deo salvatóre meo,	He looks on his servant in her lowliness;
quia respéxit humilitátem ancíllæ suæ.	henceforth all generations will call me blessed.
Ecce enim ex hoc beátam me dicent omnes generatiónes,	The Almighty works marvels for me, holy his name!
quia fecit mihi magna, qui potens est,	His mercy is from age to age, on those who fear him.
et sanctum nomen eius,	

et misericórdia eius
   in progénies
et progénies timéntibus eum.
Fecit poténtiam
   in bráchio suo,
dispérsit supérbos mente
   cordis sui;
depósuit poténtes de sede
et exaltávit húmiles.
Esuriéntes implévit bonis
et dívites dimísit inánes.
Suscépit Ísrael púerum suum,
recordátus misericórdiæ,
sicut locútus est
   ad patres nostros,
Ábraham et sémini eius
   in sæcula.
Glória patri et fílio
et spirítui sancto.
Sicut erat in princípio,
et nunc et semper,
et in sæcula sæculórum.
Amen.

He puts forth his arm
   in strength
and scatters the
   proud hearted.
He casts the mighty
   from their thrones
and raises the lowly.
He fills the starving
   with good things,
sends the rich away empty.
He protects Israel,
   his servant, remembering
   his mercy,
the mercy promised
   to our fathers,
to Abraham and his sons
   for ever.
Glory be to the Father
   and to the Son
and to the Holy Spirit.
As it was in the beginning,
   is now, and ever shall be,
world without end. Amen.

Hail Holy Queen - Salve, Regina

Attributed to several sources, the probable author is Herman the Lame (1013-1054), a monk of Reichenau Abbey in Germany.

Salve, Regína, mater
   misericórdiæ,
vita, dulcédo et spes nostra,
   salve.
Ad te clamámus,
   éxsules fílii evæ.
Ad te suspirámus geméntes
   et flentes
in hac lacrimárum valle.
eia ergo, advocáta nostra,
illos tuos misericórdes
   óculos ad nos convérte.
Et Iesum benedíctum
   fructum ventris tui,
nobis, post hoc exsílium,
   osténde.
O clemens, O pia,
   O dulcis Virgo María!

V. Ora pro nobis,
   Sancta Dei Genitrix.
R. Ut digni efficiamur
   promissionibus Christi.

Hail, holy Queen,
   Mother of mercy,
hail, our life, our sweetness
   and our hope.
To thee do we cry, poor
   banished children of Eve:
to thee do we send up
   our sighs, mourning
and weeping in this vale
   of tears.
Turn then, most gracious
   Advocate,
thine eyes of mercy toward us,
and after this our exile,
show unto us the blessed
   fruit of thy womb, Jesus,
O clement, O loving,
   O sweet Virgin Mary!

V. Pray for us, O holy
   Mother of God.
R. That we may be made
   worthy of the promises
   of Christ.

Memorare

The Memorare is a famous Marian prayer attributed to St Bernard (1090-1153)

Memoráre, o piíssima
  Virgo María,
non esse audítum a sæculo,
quemquam ad tua
  curréntem præsídia,
tua implorántem auxília,
tua peténtem suffrágia
  esse derelíctum.
Ego tali animátus
  confidéntia
ad te, Virgo Vírginum, Mater,
curro, ad te vénio,
coram te gemens
  peccátor assísto.
Noli, Mater Verbi,
  verba mea despícere,
sed audi propitia et exáudi.
  Amen.

Remember, O most
  gracious Virgin Mary,
that never was it known
  that anyone who fled
  to thy protection,
implored thy help, or sought
  thy intercession,
  was left unaided.
Inspired by this confidence
  I fly unto thee, O Virgin
  of virgins, my Mother.
To thee do I come,
  before thee I stand,
  sinful and sorrowful.
O Mother of the Word
  Incarnate, despise
  not my petitions,
but in thy mercy hear
  and answer me. Amen.

The Angelus

The custom of saying the Angelus three times a day, at 6 a.m., noon and 6 p.m. goes back to the thirteenth century.

V. Angelus Dómini nuntiávit Maríæ,
R. Et concépit de Spíritu Sancto.
Ave María...

V. Ecce ancilla Domini.
R. Fiat mihi secúndum verbum tuum.
Ave María...

V. Et Verbum caro factum est,
R. Et habitávit in nobis.
Ave María...

V. Ora pro nobis, sancta Dei Génetrix,
R. Ut digni efficiámur promissiónibus Christi.

Orémus.
Grátiam tuam, quaésumus, Dómine, méntibus nostris infúnde;

V. The angel of the Lord declared unto Mary,
R. And she conceived of the Holy Spirit.
Hail Mary...

V. Behold the handmaid of the Lord.
R. Be it done to me according to thy word.
Hail Mary...

V. And the word was made flesh,
R. And dwelt among us.
Hail Mary...

V. Pray for us O holy Mother of God,
R. That we may be made worthy of the promises of Christ.

Let us pray.
Pour forth, we beseech thee O Lord,
thy grace into our hearts

ut qui, ángelo nuntiánte,
Christi Fílii tui incarnatiónem
    cognóvimus,
per passiónem eius et crucem
ad resurrectiónis
    glóriam perducámur.
Per eúndem Christum
    Dóminum nostrum.
R. Amen.

that we to whom
    the incarnation of Christ,
    thy son,
was made known by the
    message of an angel,
may by his passion and cross
be brought to the glory of
    his resurrection
through the same Christ,
    Our Lord.
R. Amen.

PRAYERS FROM THE MISSAL AND BREVIARY

The Holy Family of Jesus, Mary and Joseph

This feast commemorates the unity and love of Jesus, Mary his mother and Joseph, his foster father, as lived out in Bethlehem, Egypt, and Nazareth, and promotes the life they lived as the ideal of family life which all Christian families should seek to emulate.

It is celebrated on the Sunday within the Octave of the Nativity of the Lord, or, if there is no Sunday on 30 December.

Collect from the Missal

O God, who were pleased to give us
the shining example of the Holy Family,
graciously grant that we may imitate them
in practising the virtues of family life
    and in the bonds of charity,
and so, in the joy of your house,
delight one day in eternal rewards.
Through our Lord Jesus Christ, your Son,
who lives and reigns with you in the unity of the Holy Spirit,
one God, for ever and ever.

Concluding Prayer from the Liturgy of the Hours

God our Father,
in the Holy Family of Nazareth
you have given us the true model of a Christian home.
   Grant that by following Jesus, Mary and Joseph
in their love for each other and in the example
   of their family life
we may come to your home of peace and joy.

1 January - Solemnity of Mary, the Holy Mother of God

This feast of the Blessed Virgin Mary, the Theotokos, or Mother of God, is held on the first day of the New Year, the Octave day of Christmas. It celebrates Mary's motherhood of Jesus, and the term Theotokos or God-bearer was adopted by the First Council of Ephesus (431), in order to safeguard the Divinity and humanity of Christ.

Collect from the Missal

O God, who through the fruitful virginity of Blessed Mary
bestowed on the human race
the grace of eternal salvation,
grant, we pray,
that we may experience the intercession of her,
through whom we were found worthy
to receive the author of life,
our Lord Jesus Christ, your Son.

Who lives and reigns with you
   in the unity of the Holy Spirit,
one God, for ever and ever.

2 February - the Presentation of the Lord

The Presentation of the Lord, popularly known as 'Candlemas,' traditionally concludes the celebration of the season of Christmas. It commemorates the presentation of Jesus in the Temple by Our Lady and St Joseph, forty days after his birth, an occasion when offerings were made and the mother was ritually purified.

Collect from the Missal

Almighty ever-living God,
we humbly implore your majesty
that, just as your Only Begotten Son
was presented on this day in the Temple
in the substance of our flesh,
so, by your grace,
we may be presented to you with minds made pure.
Through our Lord Jesus Christ, your Son,
who lives and reigns with you
   in the unity of the Holy Spirit,
one God, for ever and ever.

11 February - Our Lady of Lourdes

The feast marks the first apparition of the Blessed Virgin Mary in 1858 to fourteen-year-old St Bernadette Soubirous. There were eighteen apparitions in all, the last of which was on 16 July 1858. The message of Lourdes is a call to personal conversion, prayer and charity. In a special way, the shrine has become closely associated with the sick.

Collect from the Missal

Grant us, O merciful God, protection in our weakness,
that we, who keep the Memorial of the Immaculate
   Mother of God,
may, with the help of her intercession,
rise up from our iniquities.
Through our Lord Jesus Christ, your Son,
who lives and reigns with you
   in the unity of the Holy Spirit,
one God, for ever and ever.

Concluding prayer from the Liturgy of the Hours

Lord of mercy,
as we keep the memory of Mary,
the immaculate Mother of God,
who appeared to Bernadette at Lourdes:
grant us through her prayer
strength in our weakness
and grace to rise up from our sins.
(We make our prayer) through our Lord.

19 March - Solemnity of St Joseph, Spouse of the Blessed Virgin Mary

Although no words of St Joseph are recorded in Sacred Scripture, he has come to be regarded as one of the greatest and most popular saints, largely because of his humility and his closeness to Our Lord. He died before the beginning of Jesus' public ministry and, since he probably died in the presence of Jesus and Mary, is venerated as the patron of a good death. Blessed Pius IX named him patron of the universal church and Blessed John XXIII added his name to the Roman Canon of the Mass.

Collect from the Missal

Grant, we pray, almighty God,
that by Saint Joseph's intercession
your Church may constantly watch over
the unfolding of the mysteries of human salvation,
whose beginnings you entrusted to his faithful care.
Through our Lord Jesus Christ, your Son,
who lives and reigns with you in the unity of the Holy Spirit,
one God, for ever and ever.

Concluding prayer from the Liturgy of the Hours

Almighty God,
at the beginnings of our salvation,
when Mary conceived your Son and brought him forth
   into the world,
you placed them under Joseph's watchful care.

May his prayer still help your Church
to be an equally faithful guardian of your mysteries
and a sign of Christ to mankind.
Through Christ our Lord. Amen.

25 March - Solemnity of The Annunciation of the Lord

On the floor of the Holy House in Nazareth, an inscription reads 'Verbum caro hic factum est'; 'the Word was made flesh here'. When the Blessed Virgin said 'yes' to the Angel Gabriel, the Word became flesh; the child conceived on this day was born nine months later on Christmas Day to die for our sins and conquer death.

Collect from the Missal

O God, who willed that your Word
should take on the reality of human flesh
in the womb of the Virgin Mary,
grant, we pray,
that we, who confess our Redeemer to be God and man,
may merit to become partakers even in his divine nature.
Who lives and reigns with you
   in the unity of the Holy Spirit,
one God, for ever and ever.

Concluding Prayer from the Liturgy of the Hours

Shape us in the likeness of the divine nature
   of our Redeemer,
whom we believe to be true God and true man,
since it was your will, Lord God,
that he, your Word,
should take to himself our human nature
in the womb of the Blessed Virgin Mary.
(We make our prayer) through our Lord.

13 May - Our Lady of Fatima

The Blessed Virgin Mary appeared to three shepherd children at Fatima (Portugal) on the thirteenth day for six consecutive months in 1917. She brought a message of peace and reparation for sin, encouraging devotion to her Immaculate Heart, the recitation of the Holy Rosary, and the Five First Saturdays devotion of reparation.

Collect from the Missal

O God, who chose the Mother of your Son
   to be our Mother also,
grant us that, persevering in penance and prayer
for the salvation of the world,
we may further more effectively each day the reign
   of Christ.
Who lives and reigns with you
   in the unity of the Holy Spirit,
one God, for ever and ever.

31 May - the Visitation of the Blessed Virgin Mary

The Visitation commemorates the meeting between Mary and her cousin St Elizabeth at Ein Kerem, just outside Jerusalem. Feeling the presence of his Divine Saviour, St John the Baptist leapt in his mother's womb on the Blessed Virgin's arrival. Following St Elizabeth's words of greeting, Our Lady proclaimed the Magnificat, a hymn praising the Lord for all that He had done for His handmaid and expressing her attitude of faith and humility.

Collect from the Missal

Almighty ever-living God,
who, while the Blessed Virgin Mary was carrying
    your Son in her womb,
inspired her to visit Elizabeth,
grant us, we pray,
that, faithful to the promptings of the Spirit,
we may magnify your greatness
with the Virgin Mary at all times.
Through our Lord Jesus Christ, your Son,
who lives and reigns with you in the unity of the Holy Spirit,
one God, for ever and ever.

Concluding Prayer from the Liturgy of the Hours

Almighty, ever-living God,
you inspired the Blessed Virgin Mary,
when she was carrying your Son,
to visit Elizabeth.

Grant that, always docile to the voice of the Spirit,
we may, together with our Lady, glorify your Name.
(We make our prayer) through our Lord.

The Immaculate Heart of the Blessed Virgin Mary
(Saturday following the Second Sunday after Pentecost)

Devotion to the Immaculate Heart of Mary originated with St John Eudes in the seventeenth century and developed in parallel to devotion to the Sacred Heart of Jesus. Whereas the Sacred Heart shows the infinite love of God for mankind, Mary's Immaculate Heart presents us with a model for how we should love God. Honouring her Immaculate Heart not only rightly acknowledges her unique privileges but also leads us to her Son.

Collect from the Missal

O God, who prepared a fit dwelling place
   for the Holy Spirit
in the Heart of the Blessed Virgin Mary,
graciously grant that through her intercession
we may be a worthy temple of your glory.
Through our Lord Jesus Christ, your Son,
who lives and reigns with you
   in the unity of the Holy Spirit,
one God, for ever and ever.

16 July - Our Lady of Mount Carmel

This feast honours the Blessed Virgin as patroness of the Carmelite Order, which originated on Mt Carmel in Israel. It later came to be associated with a vision of St Simon Stock, said to have taken place on 16 July 1251. Wearing the 'Brown Scapular', a symbol of the Carmelite habit, is a sign of trust in Mary's maternal help, especially at the hour of death.

Collect from the Missal

May the venerable intercession of the glorious Virgin Mary
come to our aid, we pray, O Lord,
so that, fortified by her protection,
we may reach the mountain which is Christ.
Who lives and reigns with you
   in the unity of the Holy Spirit,
one God, for ever and ever.

26 July - Saints Joachim and Anne, Parents of the Blessed Virgin Mary

Saints Joachim and Anne were the parents of the Blessed Virgin Mary and the grandparents of the Lord. They remind us that the Word truly became flesh in a particular family. Our devotion to them is an extension of our love of Mary and her Divine Son.

Collect from the Missal

O Lord, God of our Fathers,
who bestowed on Saints Joachim and Anne this grace,
that of them should be born the Mother
   of your incarnate Son,
grant, through the prayers of both,
that we may attain the salvation
you have promised to your people.
Through our Lord Jesus Christ, your Son,
who lives and reigns with you
   in the unity of the Holy Spirit,
one God, for ever and ever.

5 August - the Dedication of the Basilica of Saint Mary Major

In the early fifth century, Pope Sixtus III dedicated the restored Basilica of St Mary Major in Rome to Mary, Mother of God. According to tradition its location had originally been indicated by a miraculous shower of snow on 5 August, in the middle of the Roman summer, hence the title 'Our Lady of the Snows'. The basilica is considered the most important church dedicated to the Blessed Virgin Mary and the festival of its dedication renews our links with Rome.

Collect from the Missal

Pardon the faults of your servants, we pray, O Lord,
that we, who cannot please you by our own deeds,

may be saved through the intercession
of the Mother of your Son and our Lord.
Who lives and reigns with you
   in the unity of the Holy Spirit,
one God, for ever and ever.

15 August - the Assumption of the Blessed Virgin Mary

The Solemnity of the Assumption is, in some ways, the paramount feast of Our Lady, since it commemorates her passing, body and soul, into glory in Heaven, where she stands beside her Son 'in garments of gold'. The dogma of the Assumption was only defined in 1950, but it was widely believed by the earliest Christians. The Blessed Virgin truly leads the way; she fulfilled her vocation in humility and, given her Immaculate Conception, the grave was no place for her body. Where she is now, we one day hope to be.

Vigil Mass

Collect from the Missal

O God, who, looking on the lowliness
   of the Blessed Virgin Mary,
raised her to this grace,
that your Only Begotten Son was born of her
   according to the flesh
and that she was crowned this day with surpassing glory,
grant through her prayers,
that, saved by the mystery of your redemption,
we may merit to be exalted by you on high.

Through our Lord Jesus Christ, your Son,
who lives and reigns with you
   in the unity of the Holy Spirit,
one God, for ever and ever.

Mass during the Day

Collect from the Missal

Almighty ever-living God,
who assumed the Immaculate Virgin Mary,
   the Mother of your Son,
body and soul into heavenly glory,
grant, we pray,
that, always attentive to the things that are above,
we may merit to be sharers of her glory.
Through our Lord Jesus Christ, your Son,
who lives and reigns with you
   in the unity of the Holy Spirit,
one God, for ever and ever.

Concluding Prayer from the Liturgy of the Hours

Almighty, ever-living God,
you have taken the mother of your Son,
the immaculate Virgin Mary,
body and soul into the glory where you dwell.
Keep our hearts set on heaven
so that, with her, we may share in your glory.
(We make our prayer) through our Lord.

17 August - Our Lady of Knock

In August 1879, fifteen people witnessed an apparition of Our Lady, St Joseph and St John the Evangelist, together with the Lord (as the Lamb of God), outside the church at Knock, in Ireland. It grew into an international shrine and was visited by Blessed John Paul II in 1979.

Collect from the Missal

O God, who give hope to your people in time of distress,
grant that we who keep the memorial
of the Blessed Virgin, Our Lady of Knock,
may, through her intercession,
be steadfast in the faith during our earthly pilgrimage
   to heaven,
and so come to eternal glory with all the Angels
   and the Saints.
Through our Lord Jesus Christ, your Son,
who lives and reigns with you
   in the unity of the Holy Spirit,
one God, for ever and ever.

22 August - the Queenship of the Blessed Virgin Mary

Pope Pius XII instituted this Feast in 1954, to conclude what was then the Octave of the Assumption. We remember that the Blessed Virgin reigns in Heaven, together with her Son; she reigns not because she is equal to God but because she is mother of Christ the King. All her privileges come from her Motherhood of God and the unique role she played in our redemption.

Collect from the Missal

O God, who made the Mother of your Son
to be our Mother and our Queen,
graciously grant that, sustained by her intercession,
we may attain in the heavenly Kingdom
the glory promised to your children.
Through our Lord Jesus Christ, your Son,
who lives and reigns with you
　in the unity of the Holy Spirit,
one God, for ever and ever.

8 September - the Nativity of the Blessed Virgin Mary

Nothing is known for sure about the details of the Blessed Virgin's birth, and her parents, traditionally known as St Joachim and St Anne, are not mentioned in Sacred Scripture. Today's feast originated in the East, probably during the sixth century, and was later introduced to the West. Her earthly birth is celebrated (like that of St John the Baptist) because it announced to the world the coming of Jesus, the beginning of the New Covenant.

Collect from the Missal

Impart to your servants, we pray, O Lord,
the gift of heavenly grace,
that the Feast of the Nativity of the Blessed Virgin
may bring deeper peace
to those for whom the birth of her Son
was the dawning of salvation.
Through our Lord Jesus Christ, your Son,
who lives and reigns with you
   in the unity of the Holy Spirit,
one God, for ever and ever.

12 September - the Most Holy Name of Mary

The name of Mary is regarded as holy because it is the name of the Mother of God, her who brought the Saviour into the world. The Feast of the Most Holy Name of Mary was added to the Universal Calendar in 1684 by Blessed Innocent XI, commemorating the defeat of the Turks at the gates of Vienna the previous year: a powerful example of the might of the Blessed Virgin's intercession.

Collect from the Missal

Grant, we pray, almighty God,
that, for all who celebrate the glorious Name
of the Blessed Virgin Mary,
she may obtain your merciful favour.

Through our Lord Jesus Christ, your Son,
who lives and reigns with you
   in the unity of the Holy Spirit,
one God, for ever and ever.

15 September - Our Lady of Sorrows

This feast originated as a memorial of the Seven Sorrows of Mary, most of which were linked to the events of Good Friday, when she stood at the foot of the cross. We remember that the Blessed Virgin had to live through the personal tragedy of seeing her Son die. She had a unique share in our redemption, offering her Son's life to the Lord, trusting that it was part of his plan.

Collect from the Missal

O God, who willed
that, when your Son was lifted high on the Cross,
his Mother should stand close by and share his suffering,
grant that your Church,
participating with the Virgin Mary in the Passion of Christ,
may merit a share in his Resurrection.
Who lives and reigns with you in the
   unity of the Holy Spirit,
one God, for ever and ever.

24 September - Our Lady of Walsingham

England's premier Marian shrine dates back to 1061, when a wealthy widow, Richeldis de Faverches, was inspired by a vision to build a replica of the Holy House of Nazareth in Walsingham, Norfolk. This remained a vibrant pilgrimage centre until its destruction in 1538, although the shrine was later revived by both Catholics (1897) and Anglicans (1922). Formerly, 24 September was kept as the Memorial of Our Lady of Ransom, when prayers were offered for the 'ransom' of England, 'Our Lady's Dowry.'

Collect from the Missal

Grant, we pray, almighty God,
that as in the mystery of the Incarnation
the Blessed and ever Virgin Mary
conceived your Son in her heart
before she conceived him in the womb,
so we, your pilgrim people,
rejoicing in her motherly care,
may welcome him into our hearts
and become a holy house fit for his eternal dwelling.
Who lives and reigns with you
    in the unity of the Holy Spirit,
one God, for ever and ever.

7 October - Our Lady of the Rosary

This Memorial (originally Our Lady of Victories) commemorates the battle of Lepanto (7 October 1571), when a Christian fleet defeated the Turks. The victory was attributed by Pope St Pius V to the recitation of the Holy Rosary. This great Marian prayer is traced back to St Dominic and his confrères, preaching against the Albigensian heresy in the thirteenth century, but it reached its familiar form in the fifteenth century. Since then it has spread all over the world and has produced marvellous fruits, bringing countless Christians 'to Jesus through Mary.'

Collect from the Missal

Pour forth, we beseech you, O Lord,
your grace into our hearts,
that we, to whom the Incarnation of Christ your Son
was made known by the message of an Angel,
may, through the intercession of the Blessed Virgin Mary,
by his Passion and Cross
be brought to the glory of his Resurrection.
Who lives and reigns with you
   in the unity of the Holy Spirit,
one God, for ever and ever.

21 November - The Presentation of the Blessed Virgin Mary

The Presentation of Mary in the Temple as a young girl is based not on the New Testament but on an account in the apocryphal Protoevangelium of James. In doing this, the Blessed Virgin dedicated herself to the service of God and was thus open to God's will. The feast prepares us for Advent and Christmas, when we celebrate the coming of her Divine Son into the world.

Collect from the Missal

As we venerate the glorious memory
of the most holy Virgin Mary,
grant, we pray, O Lord, through her intercession,
that we, too, may merit to receive
from the fullness of your grace.
Through our Lord Jesus Christ, your Son,
who lives and reigns with you
   in the unity of the Holy Spirit,
one God, for ever and ever.

8 December - Solemnity of the Immaculate Conception of the Blessed Virgin Mary

This Solemnity celebrates the Blessed Virgin's unique privilege of being preserved from the stain of sin at the very moment of her conception. This was fitting for she would one day carry the second person of the Trinity in her womb. But with Mary, the manner in which she was saved was exceptional: from the first moment of her existence, she was free from the stain of Original Sin. This dogma was solemnly defined by Blessed Pius IX on 8 December 1854 but had long been widely believed by Christians.

Collect from the Missal

O God, who by the Immaculate Conception
   of the Blessed Virgin
prepared a worthy dwelling for your Son,
grant, we pray,
that, as you preserved her from every stain
by virtue of the Death of your Son, which you foresaw,
so, through her intercession,
we, too, may be cleansed and admitted to your presence.
Through our Lord Jesus Christ, your Son,
who lives and reigns with you
   in the unity of the Holy Spirit,
one God, for ever and ever.

12 December - Our Lady of Guadalupe

On 9 December 1531, the Blessed Virgin Mary appeared to St Juan Diego and left an image of herself imprinted upon his cloak. The image was placed in a magnificent shrine where it became an object of great devotion and encouraged the conversion of the Mexican people to Christ.

Many miracles were attributed to her intercession and Our Lady of Guadalupe was named as 'Queen of Mexico and Empress of the Americas'.

Collect from the Missal

O God, Father of mercies,
who placed your people under the singular protection
of your Son's most holy Mother,
grant that all who invoke the Blessed Virgin of Guadalupe,
may seek with ever more lively faith
the progress of peoples in the ways of justice and of peace.
Through our Lord Jesus Christ, your Son,
who lives and reigns with you
   in the unity of the Holy Spirit,
one God, for ever and ever.

25 December - The Nativity of the Lord, Christmas Day

Christmas Day is the culmination of the Advent Season, and the glorious commemoration of the Birth of Our Lord Jesus Christ of the Blessed Virgin Mary. His birth was foretold by the prophets, and long awaited. Our Lady and St Joseph travelled to Bethlehem for a census, and it was here that Jesus was born. But it happened in silence, poverty and humility, and the first people to see the Infant Christ were poor shepherds.

At the Mass during the Day

Collect from the Missal

O God, who wonderfully created the dignity of human nature
and still more wonderfully restored it,
grant, we pray,
that we may share in the divinity of Christ,
who humbled himself to share in our humanity.
Who lives and reigns with you
   in the unity of the Holy Spirit,
one God, for ever and ever.

Concluding Prayer from the Liturgy of the Hours

God our Father,
our human nature is the wonderful work of your hands,
made still more wonderful by your work of redemption.
Your Son took to himself our manhood,
grant us a share in the godhead of Jesus Christ,
who lives and reigns with you and the Holy Spirit,
God for ever and ever.

THE ROSARY OF THE BLESSED VIRGIN MARY

Introduction

The Rosary of the Virgin Mary, which gradually took shape in the second millennium under the guidance of the Spirit of God, is a prayer loved by countless Saints and encouraged by the Magisterium. Simple yet profound, it still remains a prayer of great significance, destined to bring forth a harvest of holiness, yet it blends easily into the spiritual journey of the Christian life.

The Rosary, though clearly Marian in character, is at heart a Christocentric prayer. In the sobriety of its elements, it has all the depth of the Gospel message in its entirety, of which it can be said to be a compendium. It is an echo of the prayer of Mary, her perennial *Magnificat* for the work of the redemptive Incarnation which began in her virginal womb.

With the Rosary, the Christian people sits in the school of Mary and is led to contemplate the beauty on the face of Christ and to experience the depths of his love. Through the Rosary the faithful receive abundant grace, as though from the very hands of the Mother of the Redeemer.

(Adapted from the Apostolic Letter, *Rosarium Virginis Mariæ*, "The Rosary of the Virgin Mary," Pope John Paul II, 2002)

The Holy Rosary

"The Rosary is a gospel prayer. The orderly and gradual unfolding of the Rosary reflects the very way in which the Word of God, mercifully entering into human affairs, brought about redemption." (Pope Paul VI, *Marialis Cultus*, 1974, n. 44)

The Holy Rosary is now, following the introduction of five new "luminous" mysteries by Pope John Paul II in 2002, composed of twenty "decades", each comprising the Our Father, ten Hail Marys, and a Glory Be, recited in honour of some mystery in the life of Our Lord or his Blessed Mother. We pray to practise the virtue specially taught by that mystery, and the Holy Rosary is both meditation and supplication, since the prayers are said while the mind and heart dwell on particular incidents of the life and death of our Lord Jesus Christ and his mother, Mary.

The Mysteries of the Rosary

These incidents in the lives of Jesus and Mary are set out in twenty named "mysteries". These are presented in four groups of five "mysteries" each, remembering many significant events from the Gospels and of our salvation story. (See list on pp. 43-44)

Thus there are five "Joyful Mysteries" marked by the joy radiating from the event of the Incarnation, recalling the infancy and hidden ministry of Jesus. There are five "Mysteries of Light" (or "Luminous Mysteries"), recalling how Jesus, in the years of his public life and proclaiming the kingdom of God, truly emerges as "the light of the world". Then there are five "Sorrowful Mysteries", which focus on the individual moments of the Passion and Death of our Lord, revealing the culmination of God's love for us. Finally, there are five "Glorious Mysteries", which invite us to pass beyond death in order to gaze upon Christ's glory in the new life of the resurrection, and to relive the joy of the apostles and of Mary. In so doing we rediscover the reasons for our own faith.

Praying the Mysteries of the Rosary

To pray the Rosary usually means to pray five "decades" of the Rosary, and so involves saying the Our Father, followed by ten Hail Marys and then the Glory Be – this is repeated five times altogether. While marking each prayer that is being said by passing the beads through the fingers, time is given to meditating on the particular theme attached to each of the "decades" being prayed. These themes are described in the five mysteries chosen, whether the Joyful, Luminous, Sorrowful or Glorious mysteries. If you chose the Joyful Mysteries, for example, the first of the five mysteries, the Annunciation, is the theme to meditate on during the first decade. The second mystery, the Visitation, attaches to the second decade, and so on until the fifth mystery and decade.

Aids to saying the Rosary

Announcing each "mystery" is important, as the words direct the imagination and mind towards a particular episode in the life of Christ, opening up a scenario to focus our attention. It is often helpful to use icons, holy images, or a rosary booklet, to concentrate the mind, and corresponds to the inner logic of the Incarnation. It is also most helpful to follow the announcement with the proclamation of a relevant scripture passage, providing a biblical foundation and greater depth to our meditation. So God is allowed to speak and we listen in silence.

Mysteries said on certain days

Traditionally, different Mysteries of the Rosary have been allocated to different days of the week. There are no strict rules, but a recommended practice is as follows:

The Joyful Mysteries to be said on Mondays and Saturdays.
The Mysteries of Light on Thursdays.
The Sorrowful Mysteries on Tuesdays and Fridays.
The Glorious Mysteries on Wednesdays and Sundays.

Customary changes to this pattern may arise during certain liturgical seasons of the year. So for example on the Sundays during Advent and Christmastide the Joyful Mysteries are often said, and in a similar way, the Sorrowful Mysteries on Sundays during Lent.

Beginning and ending the Rosary

The Rosary is often begun with an Our Father and three Hail Marys for the intentions of the Pope, on the set of beads next to the crucifix, as if to expand the vision of the one praying to embrace all the needs of the Church. To encourage this ecclesial dimension of the Rosary, the Church has seen fit to grant indulgences to those who recite it with the required dispositions.

Since the Rosary is truly a spiritual itinerary in which Mary acts as Mother, Teacher and Guide, it concludes with the opportunity to praise of the Blessed Virgin by praying either the "Hail Holy Queen" (*Salve Regina*) or the Litany of Loreto. The choice of some of these prayers is guided by the liturgical season.

To conclude: to pray the Rosary is nothing other than to contemplate with Mary the face of Christ.

The twenty mysteries are:

The Five Joyful Mysteries

1. The Annunciation (*Lk* 1:26-38).
2. The Visitation (*Lk* 1:39-45).
3. The Nativity (*Lk* 2:1-7).
4. The Presentation in the Temple (*Lk* 2:22-35).
5. The Finding of the Child Jesus in the Temple (*Lk* 2:41-52).

The Five Mysteries of Light

1. The Baptism in the Jordan (*Mt* 3:13-17).
2. The Wedding at Cana (*Jn* 2:1-12).
3. The Proclamation of the Kingdom of God (*Mk* 1:14-15; 2:3-12).
4. The Transfiguration (*Lk* 9:28-36).
5. The Institution of the Eucharist (*Mt* 26:26-29).

The Five Sorrowful Mysteries

1. The Prayer and Agony in the Garden (*Mk* 14:32-42).
2. The Scourging at the Pillar (*Mt* 27:15-26).
3. The Crowning with Thorns (*Mt* 27:27-31).
4. The Carrying of the Cross (*Jn* 19:15-17; *Lk* 23:27-32).
5. The Crucifixion and Death of Our Lord (*Lk* 23:33-38, 44-46).

The Five Glorious Mysteries

1. The Resurrection (*Mt* 28:1-8).
2. The Ascension of Christ into Heaven (*Ac* 1:6-11).
3. The Descent of the Holy Spirit on the Apostles (*Ac* 2:1-12).
4. The Assumption (*2 Th* 4:13-19).
5. The Coronation of the Blessed Virgin Mary in Heaven and the Glory of all the Saints (*Rv* 12:1; 14:1-5: *Is* 6:1-3).

How to Say the Rosary

If you have a set of Rosary beads, first kiss the crucifix, then make the sign of the cross and then with the crucifix say the Apostles' Creed. Then on the first bead above the crucifix say the Lord's Prayer, the Our Father. This is the prayer which Jesus taught his apostles when they asked him to show them how to pray (see *Mt* 6:19 and *Lk* 11:2-4). Then on each of the three following beads say the Hail Mary. Traditionally these three Hail Marys are said for the intentions of the Holy Father. Then say the Glory Be.

On the same bead then say the Lord's Prayer, the Our Father. This is followed by ten Hail Marys on the next ten beads, and the decade is concluded with a Glory Be. And then it has become traditional to say the prayer given to the children at Fatima on 13 July 1917 at the end of each decade:

> O my Jesus, forgive us our sins, save us from the fires of hell, and lead all souls to Heaven, especially those in most need of Thy mercy.

In fact, at each of the six apparitions of Our Lady to the seers at Fatima, between May and October 1917, she asked them to pray the Rosary daily, for the end of violence in the world and a time of peace. She also described herself as the Lady of the Rosary, during these apparitions, further emphasizing its importance.

THE LITANY OF LORETO

The Litany of Loreto arose at the sanctuary of Loreto, which is situated near Ancona in Italy. It is believed that the house where the Blessed Virgin was born, and where the Angel Gabriel announced the Incarnation of the Word to her, is now situated there. According to pious tradition, the Holy House was transported by angels from the Holy Land to Italy in the late thirteenth century. Existing accounts of this event date from the late fifteenth and early sixteenth centuries. The account of the translation of the Holy House has been accepted as worthy of belief by numerous Popes, and it was visited by saints including Francis Xavier, Francis Borgia, Charles Borromeo, and Francis de Sales. The house now stands inside a Basilica which was built around it.

The Litany of Loreto follows the usual form for litanies, beginning with *Kyrie Eleison*, and then invocations of the persons of the Holy Trinity. The Blessed Virgin is then addressed as Mother, Virgin, and Queen, as well as with a variety of titles, expressing her qualities and power of intercession. Most of the titles given to Our Lady in the Litany find an echo in the works of the Fathers of the early Church. There were many litanies in use in the sixteenth century, but they were gradually superseded by the Litany of Loreto, following approval by Pope Sixtus V in 1587.

The Feast of Our Lady of Loreto is celebrated in certain dioceses on 10 December, and in 1920 Pope Benedict XV declared Our Lady of Loreto the patroness of airmen. Over time invocations have been added to the Litany, with the most recent being "Queen of the family," at the instigation of Pope John Paul II, and both he and Pope Benedict XVI have visited the shrine during their pontificates.

Litaniæ Lauretanæ

Kyrie, eleison.
Christe, eleison.
Kyrie, eleison.
Christe, audi nos.
Christe, exaudi nos.
Pater de cælis, Deus,
miserere nobis.
Fili, Redemptor mundi, Deus,
Spiritus Sancte, Deus,
Sancta Trinitas, unus Deus,
Sancta Maria,
ora pro nobis.
Sancta Dei Genetrix,
Sancta Virgo virginum,
Mater Christi,
Mater Ecclesiæ,
Mater Misericordiæ,

Litany of Loreto

Lord, have mercy.
Christ, have mercy.
Lord, have mercy.
Christ, hear us.
Christ, graciously hear us.
God the Father of heaven,
have mercy upon us.
God the Son, Redeemer of the world,
God the Holy Spirit,
Holy Trinity, one God,
Holy Mary,
pray for us.
Holy Mother of God,
Holy Virgin of virgins,
Mother of Christ,
Mother of the Church,
Mother of Mercy,

Mater divinæ gratiæ,	Mother of divine grace,
Mater Spei,	Mother of Hope,
Mater purissima,	Mother most pure,
Mater castissima,	Mother most chaste,
Mater inviolata,	Mother inviolate,
Mater intemerata,	Mother undefiled,
Mater amabilis,	Mother most amiable,
Mater admirabilis,	Mother most admirable,
Mater boni consilii,	Mother of good counsel,
Mater Creatoris,	Mother of our Creator,
Mater Salvatoris,	Mother of our Saviour,
Virgo prudentissima,	Virgin most prudent,
Virgo veneranda,	Virgin most venerable,
Virgo prædicanda,	Virgin most renowned,
Virgo potens,	Virgin most powerful,
Virgo clemens,	Virgin most merciful,
Virgo fidelis,	Virgin most faithful,
Speculum iustitiæ,	Mirror of justice,
Sedes sapientiæ,	Seat of wisdom,
Causa nostræ lætitiæ,	Cause of our joy,
Vas spirituale,	Spiritual vessel,
Vas honorabile,	Vessel of honour,
Vas insigne devotionis,	Singular vessel of devotion,
Rosa mystica,	Mystical rose,
Turris Davidica,	Tower of David,
Turris eburnea,	Tower of ivory,
Domus aurea,	House of gold,

Fœderis arca,	Ark of the covenant,
Ianua cæli,	Gate of heaven,
Stella matutina,	Morning star,
Salus infirmorum,	Health of the sick,
Refugium peccatorum,	Refuge of sinners,
Solacium migrantium,	Solace of Migrants,
Consolatrix afflictorum,	Comfort of the afflicted,
Auxilium Christianorum,	Help of Christians,
Regina Angelorum,	Queen of angels,
Regina Patriarcharum,	Queen of patriarchs,
Regina Prophetarum,	Queen of prophets,
Regina Apostolorum,	Queen of apostles,
Regina Martyrum,	Queen of martyrs,
Regina Confessorum,	Queen of confessors,
Regina Virginum,	Queen of virgins,
Regina Sanctorum omnium,	Queen of all saints,
Regina sine labe originali concepta,	Queen conceived without original sin,
Regina in cælum assumpta,	Queen assumed into heaven,
Regina sacratissimi Rosarii,	Queen of the most holy Rosary,
Regina familiæ,	Queen of families,
Regina pacis,	Queen of peace,

Agnus Dei, qui tollis peccata mundi,
parce nobis, Domine.

Lamb of God, who takes away the sins of the world,
spare us, O Lord.

Agnus Dei, qui tollis
   peccata mundi,
exaudi nos, Domine.
Agnus Dei, qui tollis
peccata mundi,
miserere nobis.

V. Ora pro nobis,
sancta Dei Genetrix.

R. Ut digni efficiamur
   promissionibus Christi.

Oremus.
Concede nos famulos tuos,
quæsumus, Domine Deus,
perpetua mentis et corporis
   sanitate gaudere,
et gloriosæ beatæ Mariæ
semper Virginis intercessione,
a præsenti liberari tristitia,
et æterna perfrui lætitia.
Per Christum
   Dominum nostrum.
R. Amen.

Lamb of God, who takes
   away the sins of the world,
graciously hear us, O Lord.
Lamb of God, who takes
   away the sins of the world,
have mercy upon us.

V. Pray for us,
O holy Mother of God.

R. That we may be made
   worthy of the promises
   of Christ.

Let us pray.
Grant, we beseech Thee,
O Lord God, unto us
Thy servants, that we may
rejoice in continual health
of mind and body; and,
by the glorious intercession
of blessed Mary ever
Virgin, may be delivered
from present sadness,
and enter into the joy of
Thine eternal gladness.
Through Christ our Lord.
R. Amen.

PRAYERS FROM ENGLISH SOURCES

England as the Dowry of Mary

During the Medieval period, England was known as the Dowry of Mary because of the particularly strong devotion to Our Lady which existed in the country. The word Dowry carries the idea of a special endowment or gift. By the fourteenth century, Thomas Arundel (1353-1414), the Archbishop of Canterbury could say: "We the English being the servants of her special inheritance and her own dowry, as we are commonly called, ought to surpass others in the warmth of our praise and devotion (to the Blessed Virgin Mary)."

WALSINGHAM - 1061

According to the text of the Pynson Ballad (c. 1485), the Shrine of Our Lady at Walsingham was established by Richeldis de Faverches in 1061. She had prayed to Our Lady and offered to undertake some special work in her honour. In answer, she was asked by the Blessed Virgin to build a replica at Walsingham of the Holy House in Nazareth where the Annunciation took place. The last verse of the Pynson Ballad is a prayer to Mary:

O gracyous Lady, glory of Jerusalem,
Cypresse of Syon and Joye of Israel,
Rose of Jeryco and Sterre of Bethleem,
O gloryous Lady, our askynge nat repell,
In mercy all wymen ever thou doste excell,
Therfore, blissed Lady, graunt thou thy great grace
To all that the devoutly visyte in this place.

O gracious Lady, glory of Jerusalem,
Cypress of Sion and Joy of Israel,
Rose of Jericho and Star of Bethlehem,
O glorious Lady, our asking do not repel,
In mercy all women ever thou dost excel,
Therefore, blessed Lady, grant thou thy great grace
To all that devoutly visit this place.

Prayer to Our Lady of Walsingham

O alone of all women, Mother and Virgin,
Mother most happy, Virgin most pure,
now we sinful as we are,
come to see thee who are all pure,
we salute thee, we honour thee as how we may
    with our humble offerings;
may thy Son grant us, that imitating thy most holy manners,
we also, by the grace of the Holy Spirit
may deserve spiritually to conceive the Lord Jesus
in our inmost soul, and once conceived never to lose him.
Amen.

St Aldhelm, a poet and scholar, flourished during the seventh century, and was Abbot of Malmesbury Abbey. He praised Our Lady in his poem, *In basilica beatæ Mariæ semper virginis* (c. 685)

Femina præpollens 　et sacra puerpera virgo Audi clementer populorum 　vota precantum, Marcida qui riguis umectant 　imbribus ora Ac genibus tundant curvato 　poplite terram Dum veniam fuso lacrimarum 　fonte merentur Et crebis precibus delent 　peccamina vitæ.	Excellent lady and holy 　virgin mother: listen mercifully 　to the petitions 　of these people praying, who moisten their withered 　faces with streams of tears and, on bended leg, strike 　the earth with their knees, seeing that they deserve 　forgiveness from the flowing fountain 　of their tears and obliterate the sins 　of their life with their continual prayers.

St Bede, the Venerable Bede, (672/73-735) was a monk at the monastery of St Peter in the Kingdom of Northumbria. He was a scholar and author, with his best known work being the *Historia ecclesiastica gentis Anglorum,* the "Ecclesiastical History of the English People." He composed a hymn, *In natali sanctæ Dei genitricis,* in which he praises Our Lady thus:

Pudica cuius viscera Sancto dicata Spiritu, Davidis ortum semine Regem ferebant sæculi	Whose chaste womb, consecrated to the Holy Spirit, brought forth the king of the world, born from the seed of David.
Beata cuius ubera Summo repleta munere Terris alebant unicam Terræ polique gloriam.	Whose blessed breasts, filled with the highest gift, nourished for the world the unique glory of earth and sky.

Probably the earliest vernacular praise of Our Lady is found in the work attributed to **Cynewulf**, an Anglo-Saxon poet, who probably flourished in the late eighth or early ninth centuries. In fact, the first surviving use of the term "Our Lady" in England is found in the works of Cynewulf. Here is the beginning of his work, "The Christ,"

Hail, thou glory of this middle-world!
The purest woman throughout all the earth.
Of those that were from immemorial time
How rightly art thou named by all endowed
With gifts of speech! All mortals throughout earth
Declare full blithe of heart that thou art bride
Of Him that ruleth the empyral sphere.

There is a prayer to the Blessed Virgin in the Book of Nunnaminster, an Anglo-Saxon prayer book from an Abbey at Winchester, which dates from the 9th century.

Sancta Maria gloriosa Dei genetrix et semper virgo, quæ mundo meruisti generare salutem, et lucem mundi cælorumque gloriam obtulisti sedentibus in tenebris et umbra mortis, esto mihi pia dominatrix, et cordis mei inluminatrix, et adiutrix apud Deum Patrem omnipotentem, ut veniam delictorum meorum accipere, et inferni tenebras evadere, et ad vitam æternam pervenire merear.	Glorious and ever-virgin holy Mary, mother of God, who deserved to give birth to salvation for the world and offered the light of the world and the glory of the heavens to those sitting in darkness and the shadow of death, be to me a kind patroness and enlightener of my heart and helper before God, the omnipotent Father, so that I may deserve to receive forgiveness for my offences and to escape the darkness of hell and attain to eternal life.

The Book of Cerne is a ninth century Anglo-Saxon prayer book from the kingdom of Mercia, which contains a number of Marian prayers including this one:

Sancta Dei genetrix semper virgo,	Holy, ever-virgin mother of God,
beata, benedicta, gloriosa et generosa,	happy, blessed, glorious and noble,
intacta et intemerata, casta et incontaminata Maria, inmaculata,	untouched and pure, chaste and undefiled Mary, immaculate,
electa et a Deo dilecta,	chosen and beloved by God,
singulari sanctitate prædita atque omni laude digna,	endowed with singular sanctity and worthy of all praise,
quæ es interpellatrix pro totius mundi discrimine,	who are the mediator for the whole world when faced with danger,
exaudi, exaudi, exaudi nos, sancta Maria.	hear, hear, hear us, holy Mary.
Ora pro nobis et intercede, et auxiliare ne dedigneris.	Pray and intercede for us and do not scorn to help.
Confidimus enim et pro certo scimus quia omne quod vis potes impetrare a filio tuo Domino nostro Iesu Christo.	For we trust and we know for certain that you can obtain everything that you wish from your son, our Lord Jesus Christ,
Deo omnipotente, omnium sæculorum rege,	the omnipotent God, king of all ages,
qui vivit cum Patre et Spiritu sancto in sæcula sæculorum. Amen.	who lives with the Father and the Holy Spirit without end. Amen.

A mid-eleventh century Psalter, originally from Winchcombe, in Gloucestershire, and now in Cambridge University Library, includes the following Marian prayer:

Dei genitrix domina mea beata Maria,	Mother of God, my lady, blessed Mary,
te deprecor per Christum Iesum dominum,	I pray to you through Jesus Christ our Lord,
ut miserearis mihi peccatori famulo tuo N.,	that you may have pity on me, your servant N.,
quia multiplicata sunt peccata mea super numerum arene maris,	a sinner, for my sins are multiplied above the sands of the sea
et non habeo ubi confugiam nisi ad te, domina mea, sancta Maria.	and I have no one to whom I may have recourse except you, my lady holy Mary.
Ideo flexibiliter peto ut [ad] dominum Deum nostrum pro me intercedere digneris,	Therefore, bending down, I ask that you may deign to intercede with the lord our God for me
quatenus per tuas sanctas orationes omnia peccata mea dimettere dignetur.	in order that he may deign to forgive all my sins through your holy prayers.

A small prayer book written between 1023 and 1035 for Aelfwine, the dean of Winchester, contains a prayer to Mary and the saints, which begins as follows:

Sancta virgo virginum, succurre.	Holy Virgin of virgins, help.
Sancta Dei genetrix, intercede.	Holy mother of God, intercede,
Sancta Maria cum sanctis virginibus Dei,	Holy Mary, together with the holy virgins of God,
feliciter exaudi, quæ inter Cherubim et Seraphim assumpta,	listen favourably, because you are assumed amongst the Cherubim and the Seraphim,
agnum Dei immaculatum sequeris …	you follow the immaculate lamb of God …

and it also has a litany, which includes these petitions:

Sancta Maria, ora.	Holy Mary, pray.
Sancta Maria, intercede pro me misero peccatore.	Holy Mary, intercede for me, a wretched sinner.
Sancta Maria, adiuva me in die exitus mei ex hac præsenti vita.	Holy Mary, help me on the day of departure from this present life.
Sancta Maria, adiuva me in die tribulationis meæ.	Holy Mary, help me on the day of my distress.
Sancta Dei genetrix, ora.	Holy Mother of God, pray.
Sancta virgo virginum, ora.	Holy Virgin of virgins, pray.

A companion manuscript contains four prayers to Mary, and a Marian Office. The second of these prayers is the *Oratio ad dei Genitricem*, ("Prayer to the Mother of God"), the first English prayer to make a detailed appeal, in life and at death, for Mary's help.

Oratio ad dei Genitricem

Sancta et intemerata virgo Maria, solamen et refocillatio omnium credentium, ex qua auctor nostræ salutis incarnate dignatus est, submissis te interpello suspiriis et devotissima exoro interventione, ut at proprium pro me intercedes misero et proboso filium, quatinus quicquid in meis actibus pravum ac anime sospitati est contrarium deleat et abstergat, quicquid utile proficuumque hoc plantet consolidetque, ne humani generis callidissimus adversator de meo lætetur interitu, sed tuo iuvamine expulses tristetur, meque per tua sancta suffragia taliter Christi componat gratia, ut mente pariter et corpore

Holy and pure virgin Mary, solace and reviver of all believers, of whom the author of our salvation deigned to be incarnated, I appeal to you with humble sighs and I beseech you by your most devoted intervention that you may intercede for me, a wretched and shameful man, to your own son, that he may destroy and wipe away whatsoever is shameful in my deeds and harmful to the welfare of my soul, that he may plant and make firm whatsoever is useful and beneficial, so that the most cunning opponent of the human race may not rejoice in my ruin, but, expelled with your help, may be downcast and so, through your holy

perseverem incorrupta,
humilis et mansueta,
fidei, spei caritatisque
donis fulcita prefulgidis,
omnibusque Christi ita
obtemperans iussis,
et cum mihi dies sorsque
venerit suprema, in collegio
beatorum spiritum tibi
iugiter suppeditantium
merear annumerari, te
mitissima mundi polique
regina interveniente et
Christo filio tuo annuente,
qui cum coæterno patre et
almo pneumate vivit et
gloriatur unus omnipotens
Deus per cuncta climata
sæculi. Amen.

prayers, may the grace of
Christ so reconcile me that
I may persevere incorrupt
in mind and equally in
body, humble and gentle,
supported by the brightly
shining gifts of faith, hope
and charity, and so obeying
all the commands of
Christ, that, when my final
judgement-day shall come,
I may justly merit to be
numbered in the company
of the blessed spirits,
through their assistance
and by your intervention,
Queen of the world and of
nations, and by the assent of
Christ your Son, who with
the co-eternal Father and
the Holy Spirit lives and is
glorified, one eternal God,
through all ages of ages .
Amen.

St Anselm was born at Aosta, before becoming a monk, and eventually the abbot, of Bec Abbey in Normandy. He then became archbishop of Canterbury in 1093, and held this post until his death in 1109. His works include the well known *Cur Deus Homo*, "Why God became man." He was also the author of a number of prayers to Mary, including the following extracts from his third prayer to the Mother of God.

Heart of my soul, stir yourself up as much as ever you can
(if you can do anything at all),
and let all that is within me praise the good Mary has done,
love the blessing she has received,
wonder at her loftiness, and beseech her kindness;
for I need her defence daily,
and in my need I desire, implore, and beseech it,
and if it is not according to my desire,
at least let it be above, or rather contrary to, what I deserve.

I pray to you with my whole heart
to the extent of my powers.
Hear me, Lady, answer me, most mighty helper;
let this filth be washed from my mind,
let my darkness be illuminated, my lukewarmness blaze up,
my listlessness be stirred.
For in your blessed holiness you are exalted above all,
after the highest of all, your Son,
through your omnipotent Son, with your glorious Son,
by your blessed Son.

St Simon Stock

Flos Carmeli, Flower of Carmel

Flos Carmeli, ("Flower of Carmel") is both a hymn and a prayer and is said to have been composed by St Simon Stock (c. 1165 – 1265). The Carmelite Order traces back its origins to a group of hermits who lived on Mt Carmel in the Holy Land in the twelfth century.

Flos Carmeli,
vitis florigera,
splendor cæli,
virgo puerpera singularis.
Mater mitis sed viri nescia
Carmelitis esto propitia
stella maris.
Radix Iesse germinans
flosculum nos ad esse
tecum in sæculum patiaris.
Inter spinas quæ crescis
lilium serva puras mentes
fragilium tutelaris.
Armatura fortis pugnantium
furunt bella tende
præsidium scapularis.

Flower of Carmel,
Tall vine blossom laden;
Splendour of heaven,
Childbearing yet maiden.
None equals thee.
Mother so tender,
Who no man didst know,
On Carmel's children
Thy favours bestow.
Star of the Sea.
Strong stem of Jesse,
Who bore one bright flower,
Be ever near us
And guard us each hour,
who serve thee here.

Per incerta prudens consilium per adversa iuge solatium largiaris. Mater dulcis Carmeli domina, plebem tuam reple lætitia qua bearis. Paradisi clavis et ianua, fac nos duci quo, Mater, gloria coronaris. Amen. (Alleluia.)	Purest of lilies, That flowers among thorns, Bring help to the true heart That in weakness turns and trusts in thee. Strongest of armour, We trust in thy might: Under thy mantle, Hard press'd in the fight, we call to thee. Our way uncertain, Surrounded by foes, Unfailing counsel You give to those who turn to thee. O gentle Mother Who in Carmel reigns, Share with your servants That gladness you gained and now enjoy. Hail, Gate of Heaven, With glory now crowned, Bring us to safety Where thy Son is found, true joy to see. Amen. (Alleluia.)

A fourteenth century English Benedictine monk, Thomas of Elmham, composed a Marian variation on the *Te Deum*, which is interesting because of the way it refers to England as Our Lady's Dowry:

Te ergo quæsumus Angligenis subveni quos pro Dote proprio defendisti … Salvum fac populum tuum, Domina, et a mortis peste Dotem tuam libera.	We therefore pray thee help the English people, whom thou hast defended as thine own Dowry … Save, Lady, thy people, and deliver thy Dowry from the curse of death.

Adam lay y-bounden

Adam lay y-bounden is an anonymous fifteenth century work which speaks of the Fall of Man, but also of the Redemption by Christ who was born of Mary.

Adam lay y-bounden,
Bounden in a bond;
Four thousand winter,
Thought he not too long;
And all was for an apple,
An apple that he took.
As clerkes finden written
In their book.
Ne had the apple taken been,
The apple taken been,

Ne had never Our Lady,
A been heaven's queen.
Blessed be the time
That apple taken was!
Therefore we may singen.
Deo gracias!

I syng of a mayden

"I syng of a mayden" is a medieval English composition which celebrates the Annunciation by the Angel Gabriel to Mary, and the birth of Christ.

I sing of a maiden
That is matchless,
King of all kings
For her son she chose.

He came as still
Where his mother was
As dew in April
That falls on the grass.

He came as still
To his mother's bower
As dew in April
That falls on the flower.

He came as still
Where his mother lay
As dew in April
That falls on the spray.

Mother and maiden
There was never, ever one but she;
Well may such a lady
God's mother be.

Prayer to Our Lady composed after the Reformation

Holy Mary, Mother of God,
thou dost not cease with all the saints
to pray to the Lord our God for all the needs
of the whole Catholic Church in general:
we humbly beseech thee that,
as it hath pleased thee to undertake the special protection
of this kingdom of England,
thou wilt care for the same continually
and prevail with thy Son, Jesus Christ our Lord,
that it be turned to the unity of the Catholic faith;
so that all English people, above other nations,
may henceforth call thee blessed,
and thy name for ever,
saying *Dos tua Virgo pia, per te est conversa, Maria*,
Thy dowry, blest Virgin Mary,
has been brought back by thee.

Cardinal Newman's Prayer to Our Lady

O Mother of Jesus, and my Mother, let me dwell with you,
cling to you and love you with ever-increasing love.
I promise the honour, love and trust of a child.

Give me a mother's protection,
> for I need your watchful care.

You know better than any other the thoughts and desires
> of the Sacred Heart.

Keep constantly before my mind the same thoughts,
> the same desires,

that my heart may be filled with zeal for the interests
> of the Sacred Heart of your Divine Son.

Instil in me a love of all that is noble,
that I may no longer be easily turned to selfishness.
Help me, dearest Mother,
to acquire the virtues that God wants of me:
to forget myself always, to work solely for him,
without fear of sacrifice.

I shall always rely on your help to be what Jesus wants
> me to be.

I am his; I am yours, my good Mother!
Give me each day your holy and maternal blessing
until my last evening on earth,
when your Immaculate Heart will present me to the heart
> of Jesus in heaven,

there to love and bless you and your divine Son
> for all eternity.

Prayer for England

This prayer has traditionally been said at Benediction. It is a prayer for the unity of the Church in England.

O Blessed Virgin Mary, Mother of God,
and our most gentle queen and mother,
look down in mercy upon England, your dowry,
and upon us all who greatly hope and trust in you.
By you it was that Jesus, our Saviour and our hope,
was given to the world;
and he has given you to us that we may hope still more.
Plead for us your children,
whom you received and accepted at the foot of the cross,
O mother of sorrows.
Pray for our separated brethren,
that in the one true fold of Christ,
we may all be united under the care of Pope N.,
the chief shepherd of Christ's flock.
Pray for us all, dear mother, that by faith,
and fruitful in good works,
we may all deserve to see and praise God,
together with you in our heavenly home.

PRAYERS FROM APPROVED MARIAN APPARITIONS

Guadalupe

Our Lady appeared to St Juan Diego at Tepeyac hill, near Mexico city, several times in 1531 and left the miraculous image of Guadalupe imprinted on his cloak.

Pope Saint Pius X's Prayer to Our Lady of Guadalupe

Our Lady of Guadalupe,
Mystical Rose,
make intercession for the holy Church,
protect the Sovereign Pontiff,
help all those who invoke thee in their necessities,
and since thou art the ever Virgin Mary
and Mother of the true God,
obtain for us from thy most holy Son
the grace of keeping our faith,
sweet hope in the midst of the bitterness of life,
burning charity and the precious gift of final perseverance.
Amen.

Rue du Bac

Our Lady appeared several times to St Catherine Labouré at the Rue du Bac convent in Paris, France, in 1830, asking her to have struck a medal dedicated to her Immaculate Conception.

Prayer on the Miraculous Medal

O Mary, conceived without sin,
pray for us who have recourse to thee!

LOURDES

Our Lady appeared to St Bernadette Soubirous at Lourdes, France, in 1858, with a message of prayer and penance. She revealed the miraculous spring at the Grotto, which has been a source of healing for many.

Pope John Paul II -
Prayer at the Lourdes Grotto in the Vatican Gardens

O blessed Virgin, Mother of God, Mother of Christ,
Mother of the Church, look upon us mercifully at this hour.
Faithful Virgin, pray for us.
Teach us to believe as you believed.
Make our faith in God, in Christ, in the Church,
always to be serene, courageous, strong, and generous.
Mother worthy of love.
Mother of faithful love, pray for us.
Teach us to love God and our brothers and sisters
as you loved them:
make our love for others to be always patient, kindly,
 and respectful.
Cause of our joy, pray for us.
Teach us to be able to grasp, in faith,
the paradox of Christian joy,

which springs up and blooms from sorrow, renunciation,
and union with your sacrificed Son.
Make our joy to be always genuine and full,
in order to be able to communicate it to all. Amen.

Fatima

Our Lady appeared to the three young seers, Blessed Jacinta and Blessed Francisco Marto, and Lucia dos Santos at Fatima in Portugal, between May and October of 1917, with a message of prayer and penance. On 13 October 1917, the Blessed Virgin performed the great miracle of the sun, as proof of her apparitions, and that all might believe.

Fatima Prayers

Reparation Prayer of the Angel – given to the three seers in the Autumn of 1916

O Most Holy Trinity, Father, Son and Holy Spirit,
I adore Thee profoundly.
I offer Thee the most precious Body, Blood, Soul and
    Divinity of Jesus Christ
present in all the tabernacles of the world,
in reparation for the outrages, sacrileges and indifferences
    by which He is offended.
And by the infinite merits of the Sacred Heart of Jesus
and the Immaculate Heart of Mary
I beg the conversion of poor sinners.

Sacrifice Prayer – given to the seers by Our Lady on 13 June 1917, and to be said when making a sacrifice or offering up an action in reparation.

O Jesus, it is for your love,
for the conversion of sinners,
and in reparation for sins
committed against the Immaculate Heart of Mary.

Litany of Our Lady of Fatima

Our Lady of Fatima, *pray for our dear country.*
Our Lady of Fatima, *sanctify our clergy.*
Our Lady of Fatima, *make our Catholics more fervent.*
Our Lady of Fatima, *guide and inspire those who govern us.*
Our Lady of Fatima, *cure the sick who confide in thee.*
Our Lady of Fatima, *console the sorrowful who trust in thee.*
Our Lady of Fatima, *help those who invoke your aid.*
Our Lady of Fatima, *deliver us from all dangers.*
Our Lady of Fatima, *help us to resist temptation.*
Our Lady of Fatima, *obtain for us all that
　we lovingly ask of thee.*
Our Lady of Fatima, *help those who are dear to us.*
Our Lady of Fatima, *bring back to the right road
　our erring brothers.*
Our Lady of Fatima, *give us back our ancient fervour.*
Our Lady of Fatima, *obtain for us pardon of our manifold
　sins and offences.*

Our Lady of Fatima, *bring all men to the feet
of thy Divine Child.*
Our Lady of Fatima, *obtain peace for the world.*

O Mary conceived without sin, *pray for us who have
recourse to thee.*
Immaculate Heart of Mary, *pray for us now
and at the hour of our death. Amen.*

Let us Pray: O God of infinite goodness and mercy, fill our hearts with a great confidence in Thy dear Mother, whom we invoke under the title of Our Lady of the Rosary and Our Lady of Fatima,
and grant us by her powerful intercession all the graces, spiritual and temporal, which we need.
Through Christ our Lord. Amen.

THE STORY OF KNOCK

At about 8 o'clock on the Thursday evening of the 21st of August, 1879, the Blessed Virgin Mary, St. Joseph and St. John the Evangelist appeared at the South gable of the Church at Knock, County Mayo, Ireland. Beside them and a little to the right was an altar with a cross and the figure of a lamb, around which angels hovered.

Novena to Our Lady of Knock

In the name of the Father, and of the Son, and of the Holy Spirit, Amen.

Give praise to the Father Almighty,
To His Son, Jesus Christ the Lord,
To the Spirit who lives in our hearts,
Both now and forever.
Amen.

Our Lady of Knock, Queen of Ireland, you gave hope to your people in a time of distress, and comforted them in sorrow. You have inspired countless pilgrims to pray with confidence to your divine Son, remembering His promise, "Ask and you shall receive, seek and you shall find."
Help me to remember that we are all pilgrims on the road to heaven. Fill me with love and concern for my brothers and sisters in Christ, especially those who live with me. Comfort me when I am sick, lonely or depressed. Teach me how to take part ever more reverently in the Holy Mass. Give me a greater love of Jesus in the Blessed Sacrament. Pray for me now, and at the hour of my death.
Amen.

Lamb of God, you take away the sins of the world;
Have mercy on us.
Lamb of God, you take away the sins of the world;
Have mercy on us.
Lamb of God, you take away the sins of the world;
Grant us peace.

St Joseph

Chosen by God to be
The Husband of Mary,
The Protector of the Holy Family,
The Guardian of the Church.
Protect all families
In their work and recreation
And Guard us on our journey through life
(*Repeat Lamb of God...* p.76)

St John

Beloved Disciple of the Lord,
Faithful priest.
Teacher of the Word of God.
Help us to hunger for the Word.
To be loyal to the Mass
And to love one another
(*Repeat Lamb of God...* p.76)

Our Lady of Knock	*Pray for us.*
Refuge of sinners	*Pray for us.*
Queen Assumed into Heaven	*Pray for us.*
Queen of the Rosary	*Pray for us.*
Mother of Nazareth	*Pray for us.*
Queen of Virgins	*Pray for us.*
Help of Christians	*Pray for us.*
Health of the Sick	*Pray for us.*

Queen of Peace	*Pray for us.*
Our Lady, Queen and Mother	*Pray for us.*
Our Lady, Mother of the Church	*Pray for us.*

(*Here mention your own special intentions*)

With the Angels and Saints let us pray:
Give praise to the Father Almighty,
To His Son, Jesus Christ the Lord,
To the Spirit who lives in our hearts,
Both now and forever.
Amen.

Instruction

The Rosary or Mass and Holy Communion is recommended each day.

ORTHODOX CHURCH PRAYERS

Orthodox liturgy and spirituality is characterised by a deep devotion to Mary, the Theotokos ("God-bearer" or "Mother of God").

Akathist hymn

The Akathist Hymn to the Blessed Virgin Mary, the Theotokos, is the most famous Marian devotion in the Orthodox Church. (The word Akathist *means, "not seated," i.e. standing). The reference to the city at the end relates to the siege of Constantinople, in 626, and the belief that the Blessed Virgin had saved the city. The Akathist Hymn is usually sung or chanted, and below are some extracts:*

The Archangel was sent from Heaven to cry "Rejoice!"
   to the Theotokos.
And beholding You, O Lord, taking bodily form,
he stood in awe, and with his bodiless voice
he cried aloud to her such things as these:

Rejoice, you through whom joy shall shine forth.
Rejoice, you whom the curse will vanish.
Rejoice, the Restoration of fallen Adam.
Rejoice, the Redemption of the tears of Eve.
Rejoice, O Height beyond human logic.

Rejoice, O depth invisible even to the eyes of Angels.
Rejoice, for you are the King's throne.
Rejoice, you bear Him, Who bears the universe.
Rejoice, O Star revealing the Sun.
Rejoice, O Womb of divine Incarnation.
Rejoice, you through whom creation is renewed.
Rejoice, you through whom the Creator is born a Babe.
Rejoice, O Bride Ever-Virgin.

Whilst praising your Offspring, we all praise you,
   O Theotokos,
as a living temple; for the Lord,
Who holds all things in His hand, dwelt in your womb,
and He sanctified and glorified you,
and taught all to cry to you:

Rejoice, Tabernacle of God the Word.
Rejoice, Holy one, holier than the Holies.
Rejoice, Ark made golden by the Spirit.
Rejoice, inexhaustible Treasury of Life.
Rejoice, precious Diadem of godly kings.
Rejoice, venerable Boast of faithful priests.
Rejoice, unshakeable Tower of the Church.
Rejoice, impregnable fortress of the Kingdom.
Rejoice, you through whom trophies are raised up.
Rejoice, you whom enemies are cast down.
Rejoice, Healing of my flesh.
Rejoice, Salvation of my soul.
Rejoice, O Bride Ever-Virgin.

Unto you, O Theotokos, invincible Champion, your City,
in thanksgiving ascribes the victory for the deliverance
   from sufferings.
And having your might unassailable,
free us from all dangers,
so that we may cry unto you:
Rejoice, O Bride Ever-Virgin.

Axion estin

Axion estin ("It is Truly Meet") is a Marian hymn, or *Theotokon*, which is chanted during the Divine Office, and in the liturgy, of Orthodox and Eastern rite Catholic Churches.

It is truly right to bless thee, O Theotokos,
ever blessed, and most pure, and the Mother of our God.
More honourable than the cherubim,
and beyond compare more glorious than the seraphim.
Without corruption thou gavest birth to God the Word.
True Theotokos, we magnify thee.

OTHER MARIAN PRAYERS AND DEVOTIONS

Sub tuum præsidium - We Fly to Thy Protection

This is the Church's oldest extant prayer to Our Lady, and has been found on a third century Greek papyrus

Sub tuum præsidium confugimus,
Sancta Dei Genetrix,
nostras deprecationes ne despicias
in necessitatibus nostris,
sed a periculis cunctis libera nos semper,
Virgo gloriosa et benedicta.
Amen.

We fly to thy protection,
O holy Mother of God,
despise not our petitions
in our necessities,
but deliver us always from all dangers,
O glorious and blessed Virgin.
Amen.

Sancta Maria, Succurre Miseris

This prayer was composed by Fulbert, an early eleventh century Bishop of Chartres in France. Chartres is one of the most beautiful of the medieval Cathedrals, and is said to hold the Sancta Camisa, a garment worn by the Blessed Virgin at Christ's birth.

Sancta Maria,	Holy Mary,
succurre miseris,	hasten to the aid
iuva pusillanimes,	of the afflicted,
refove flebiles,	support the fainthearted,
ora pro populo,	comfort the sorrowful,
interveni pro clero,	pray for your people,
intercede pro devoto	intercede on behalf
femineo sexu:	of the clergy,
sentiant omnes	intercede for devout women;
tuum iuvamen,	may all who celebrate
quiccumque celebrant tuam	your holy memory
sanctam commemorationem.	come to know your assistance.

Saint Francis of Assisi (1181/82 - 1226)

Hail Lady, Holy Queen,
Holy Mary Mother of God,
who art the Virgin made Church
and the One elect by the Most Holy Father of Heaven,
whom He consecrated with His Most Holy beloved Son
and with the Holy Spirit, the Paraclete;
Thou in whom was and is all fullness of grace
   and every good.

Hail His Palace;
Hail His Tabernacle;
Hail His Home.

Hail His Vestment;
Hail His Handmaid;
Hail His Mother

And hail all you holy virtues,
which through the grace and illumination
   of the Holy Spirit
are infused into the hearts of the faithful,
so that from those unfaithful
you make them faithful to God.

St Gertrude of Helfta, Saxony, (1256-1301)

Prayer of St Gertrude to Our Lady

Most chaste Virgin Mary,
by the spotless purity with which you prepared
   for the Son of God
a dwelling of delight in your virginal womb,
I beg of you to intercede for me
that I may be cleansed from every stain.
Most humble Virgin Mary,
by that most profound humility
by which you deserved to be raised high above all
   the choirs of angels and saints,
I beg of you to intercede for me
that all my sins may be expiated.
Most amiable Mary,
by that indescribable love
that united you so closely and inseparably to God,
I beg of you to intercede for me
that I may obtain an abundance of all merits. Amen.

O Jesus living in Mary

A seventeenth century composition by Charles de Condren and Jean-Jacques Olier.

O Jesus living in Mary,
come and live in Thy servants.
In the spirit of Thy holiness,
in the fullness of Thy might,
in the truth of Thy virtues,
in the perfection of Thy ways,
in the communion of Thy mysteries.
Subdue every hostile power in Thy spirit,
for the glory of the Father. Amen.

St Louis-Marie Grignion de Montfort (1673-1716)

St Louis de Montfort is a famous Marian saint and the author of several books of devotion to her, including his True Devotion to Mary.

Totus tuus ego sum, et omnia mea tua sunt, O Virgo, super omnia benedicta.	I am all yours, and all that is mine is yours, O Virgin, blessed above all.

Daily Consecration

I choose you today, Mary,
in the presence of the angels and saints of heaven,
for my Mother and Queen.

I consecrate to you, in obedience and love,
all that I am, all that I have, and all the good that I may do,
putting myself and all that belongs to me
entirely at your service,
for the greater glory of God in time and eternity.

Perpetual Novena Prayer to Our Lady, Mother of Perpetual Help

Pope Pius IX gave the title of Our Lady of Perpetual Help, (Our Lady of Perpetual Succour), to the Blessed Virgin, and it is associated with a 15th century Byzantine icon in a church dedicated to St Alphonsus Liguori, in Rome.

O Blessed Virgin Mary,
who, to inspire within us an unbounded confidence,
have desired to assume the most sweet name
   of Mother of Perpetual Help,
I beseech you,
assist me at all times and in every place;
in my temptations; after my failures;
in my difficulties; in all the woes of life,
and above all, at the moment of my death.
Grant me, O charitable Mother,
the conviction and habit of seeking recourse always in you;
for I am certain that, if I invoke you faithfully,
you shall be loyal in assisting me.

Obtain for me, then, that grace of graces,
the grace of praying to you incessantly

and with the confidence of a child,
so that, by virtue of that steadfast petition,
I may obtain your perpetual help and ultimate perseverance.
Bless me, O tender and benevolent Mother,
and pray for me, now and at the hour of my death. Amen.

St Maximilian Kolbe (1894-1941)

Collect from the Missal

O God, who filled the Priest
    and Martyr Saint Maximilian Kolbe
with a burning love for the Immaculate Virgin Mary
and with zeal for souls and love of neighbour,
graciously grant, through his intercession,
that, striving for your glory by eagerly serving others,
we may be conformed, even until death, to your Son.
Who lives and reigns with you
    in the unity of the Holy Spirit,
one God, for ever and ever.

Daily Renewal of Total Consecration

Immaculata, Queen and Mother of the Church,
I renew my consecration to you for this day and for always,
so that you might use me for the coming of the Kingdom
    of Jesus in the whole world.
To this end I offer you all my prayers,
    actions and sacrifices for this day.

Pope John XXIII (1881-1963)

Prayer on the Rosary

O Mary, you are praying for us,
you are always praying for us.
We know it, we feel it.
Oh what joy and truth, what sublime glory,
in this heavenly and human interchange of sentiments,
 words and actions, which the rosary always brings us:
the tempering of our human afflictions,
the foretaste of the peace that is not of this world,
the hope of eternal life!

Pope John XXIII - Prayer of Love for Mary

Holy Immaculate Mary,
help all who are in trouble.
Give courage to the faint-hearted, console the sad,
heal the infirm, pray for the people,
intercede for the clergy, have a special care for nuns;
may all feel, all enjoy your kind and powerful assistance,
all who now and always render and will render you honour,
and will offer you their petitions.
Hear all our prayers, O Mother, and grant them all.
We are all your children:
Grant the prayers of your children. Amen forever.

Pope Paul VI (1897-1978)

Prayer to Mary

Look down with maternal clemency, most Blessed Virgin,
 upon all your children.
Consider the anxiety of bishops who fear that their flocks
 will be tormented by a terrible storm of evils.
Heed the anguish of so many people,
fathers and mothers of families who are uncertain about
 their future and beset by hardships and cares.
Soothe the minds of those at war
 and inspire them with thoughts of peace.
Through your intercession, may God,
 the avenger of injuries, turn to mercy.
May He give back to nations the tranquillity they seek
 and bring them to a lasting age of genuine prosperity.

Marthe Robin (1902-1981)

Co-foundress of the Foyers of Charity, a movement which has more than seventy communities around the world dedicated to giving silent retreats.

Prayer to Our Lady

Beloved Mother,
you who know so well the paths of holiness and love,
teach us to lift our minds and our hearts often to God,
and to fix our respectful and loving attention on the Trinity.

And since you walk with us on the path of eternal life,
do not remain a stranger to the weak pilgrims
your charity is ready to welcome.
Turn your merciful face to us.
Draw us into your light.
Flood us with your kindnesses.
Take us into the light and the love.
Always take us further and higher
   into the splendours of heaven.
Let nothing ever trouble our peace,
nor turn us from the thought of God.
But let each minute take us further into the depths
   of the awesome mystery,
till the day when our souls—
fully receptive to the light of the divine union—
will see all things in eternal love and unity. Amen.

POPE JOHN PAUL II (1920-2005)

Prayer to Mary, Mother of the Church

Mother of the Church,
grant that the Church may enjoy freedom and peace
   in fulfilling her saving mission
and that to this end she may become mature with a new
   maturity of faith and inner unity.
Help us to overcome opposition and difficulties.
Help us to rediscover all the simplicity and dignity
   of the Christian vocation.

Grant that there may be no lack of "labourers in the Lord's vineyard."

Sanctify families. Watch over the souls of the young and the hearts of the children.

Help us to overcome the great moral threats against the fundamental spheres of life and love.

Obtain for us the grace to be continually renewed

through all the beauty of witness given to the cross and resurrection of your Son. Amen.

MARIAN HYMNS

Ave Maris Stella - Hail Thou Star of Ocean

Ave Maris Stella is a popular liturgical hymn dating back to at least the 9th century. The English translation is by Edward Caswall, (1814-1878), a convert Anglican clergyman who became an Oratorian.

Ave maris stella,	Hail thou star of ocean
Dei Mater alma,	Portal of the sky
Atque semper Virgo,	Ever virgin Mother
Felix cæli porta.	Of the Lord Most High
Sumens illud Ave	O! by Gabriel's Ave
Gabrielis ore,	Uttered long ago,
Funda nos in pace,	Eva's name reversing,
Mutans Hevæ nomen.	Established peace below
Solve vincla reis,	Break the captives' fetters,
Profer lumen cæcis:	Light on blindness pour,
Mala nostra pelle,	All our ills expelling,
Bona cuncta posce.	Every bliss implore
Monstra t(e) esse matrem:	Show thyself a Mother,
Sumat per te preces,	Offer Him our sighs,
Qui pro nobis natus,	Who for us incarnate
Tulit esse tuus.	Did not thee despise
Virgo singularis,	Virgin of all virgins
Inter omnes mitis,	To thy shelter take us,

| Nos culpis solutos, | Gentlest of the gentle |
| Mites fac et castos. | Chaste and gentle make us |

Vitam præsta puram,	Still, as on we journey,
Iter para tutum:	Help our weak endeavour,
Ut videntes Iesum,	Till with thee and Jesus
Semper collætemur.	We rejoice forever

Sit laus Deo Patri,	Through the highest heaven,
Summo Christo decus,	To the almighty Three
Spiritui Sancto,	Father, Son, and Spirit,
Tribus honor unus. Amen.	One same glory be. Amen.

Alma Redemptoris Mater

This hymn, like the Salve Regina, was probably composed by the monk Herman the Lame.

Alma Redemptoris Mater,
quæ pervia cæli porta manes,
et stella maris, succurre cadenti,
surgere qui curat, populo:
tu quæ genuisti, natura mirante,
tuum sanctum Genitorem, Virgo prius ac posterius,
Gabrielis ab ore, sumens illud Ave, peccatorum miserere.

From the first Sunday of Advent until Christmas Eve:

V. Angelus Domini nuntiavit Mariæ.

R. Et concepit de Spiritu Sancto.

From First Vespers of Christmas until the Presentation:

V. Post Partum Virgo inviolata permansisti.

R. Dei Genitrix, intercede pro nobis.

Loving Mother of our Saviour,
hear thou thy people's cry
Star of the deep and Portal of the sky!
Mother of Him who thee made from nothing made.
Sinking we strive and call to thee for aid:
Oh, by what joy which Gabriel brought to thee,
Thou Virgin first and last, let us thy mercy see.

From the first Sunday of Advent until Christmas Eve:

V. The Angel of the Lord declared unto Mary.
R. And she conceived by the Holy Spirit.

From First Vespers of Christmas until the Presentation:

V. After childbirth, O Virgin, thou didst remain inviolate.
R. O Mother of God, plead for us.

Stabat Mater

The Stabat mater dolorosa, *("the sorrowful mother stood"), is a thirteenth century Marian hymn, attributed to Jacopone da Todi. The well known English translation given here is by Edward Caswall.*

Stabat mater dolorosa
iuxta Crucem lacrimosa,
dum pendebat Filius.
	At the Cross her
	   station keeping,
	stood the mournful
	   Mother weeping,
	close to her Son to the last.

Cuius animam gementem, contristatam et dolentem pertransivit gladius.	His sorrow sharing, all His bitter anguish bearing, now at length the sword has passed.
O quam tristis et afflicta fuit illa benedicta, mater Unigeniti!	O how sad and sore distressed was that Mother, highly blest, of the sole-begotten One.
Quæ mærebat et dolebat, pia Mater, dum videbat nati pœnas inclyti.	Christ above in torment hangs, she beneath beholds the pangs of her dying glorious Son.
Quis est homo qui non fleret, matrem Christi si videret in tanto supplicio?	Is there one who would not weep, whelmed in miseries so deep, Christ's dear Mother to behold?
Quis non posset contristari Christi Matrem contemplari dolentem cum Filio?	Can the human heart refrain from partaking in her pain, in that Mother's pain untold?
Pro peccatis suæ gentis vidit Iesum in tormentis, et flagellis subditum.	Bruised, derided, cursed, defiled, she beheld her tender Child all with bloody scourges rent:
Vidit suum dulcem Natum moriendo desolatum, dum emisit spiritum.	For the sins of His own nation, saw Him hang in desolation, Till His spirit forth He sent.

Eia, Mater, fons amoris me sentire vim doloris fac, ut tecum lugeam.	O thou Mother! fount of love! Touch my spirit from above, make my heart with thine accord:

Fac, ut ardeat cor meum
in amando Christum Deum
ut sibi complaceam.
	Make me feel as thou hast felt;
	make my soul to glow
	    and melt
	with the love of Christ
	    my Lord.

Sancta Mater, istud agas,
crucifixi fige plagas
cordi meo valide.
	Holy Mother!
	    pierce me through,
	in my heart
	    each wound renew
	of my Saviour crucified:

Tui Nati vulnerati, tam dignati pro me pati, pœnas mecum divide.	Let me share with thee His pain, who for all my sins was slain, who for me in torments died.
Fac me tecum pie flere, crucifixo condolere, donec ego vixero.	Let me mingle tears with thee, mourning Him who mourned for me, all the days that I may live:
Iuxta Crucem tecum stare, et me tibi sociare in planctu desidero.	By the Cross with thee to stay, there with thee to weep and pray, is all I ask of thee to give.

Virgo virginum præclara, mihi iam non sis amara, fac me tecum plangere.	Virgin of all virgins blest!, Listen to my fond request: let me share thy grief divine;
Fac, ut portem Christi mortem, passionis fac consortem, et plagas recolere.	Let me, to my latest breath, in my body bear the death of that dying Son of thine.

Fac me plagis vulnerari,
 fac me Cruce inebriari,
 et cruore Filii.
	Wounded with His
	     every wound,
	 steep my soul till it
	     hath swooned,
	 in His very Blood away;

Flammis ne urar succensus, per te, Virgo, sim defensus in die iudicii.	Be to me, O Virgin, nigh, lest in flames I burn and die, in His awful Judgment Day.
Christe, cum sit hinc exire, da per Matrem me venire ad palmam victoriæ.	Christ, when Thou shalt call me hence, by Thy Mother my defence, by Thy Cross my victory;
Quando corpus morietur, fac, ut animæ donetur paradisi gloria. Amen.	While my body here decays, may my soul Thy goodness praise, Safe in Paradise with Thee. Amen.

Regina Cæli

Since the thirteenth century, the Regina Cæli has been used as the seasonal antiphon in honour of the Blessed Virgin after Night Prayer, and since 1743 it has replaced the Angelus in the Easter Season.

Regína cæli, lætáre.	Queen of heaven, rejoice.
Allelúia.	Alleluia:
Quia quem meruísti portáre.	For he whom you did merit
Allelúia.	to bear. Alleluia.
Resurréxit, sicut dixit.	Has risen, as he said.
Allelúia.	Alleluia.
Ora pro nobis, Deum.	Pray for us to God. Alleluia.
Allelúia.	Rejoice and be glad,
Gaude et lætáre, Virgo María,	O Virgin Mary. Alleluia.
Allelúia.	For the Lord has truly risen.
Quia surréxit Dominus vere.	Alleluia.
Allelúia.	
Orémus:	Let us pray:
Deus, qui per resurrectiónem	O God, who gave joy
Fílii tui,	to the world
Dómini nostri Iesu Christi,	through the resurrection
mundum lætificáre dignátus	of your Son
es:	our Lord Jesus Christ,
præsta, quáesumus;	grant, we beseech you,
ut, per eius Genitrícem	that through the intercession
Vírginem Maríam,	of the Virgin Mary,

pérpetuæ capiámus
 gáudia vitæ.
Per eúndem Christum
 Dóminum nostrum.
R. Amen.

his Mother,
we may obtain the joys
 of everlasting life,
though the same Christ
 our Lord.
R. Amen.

The Holly and the Ivy

A traditional English Christmas carol

The holly and the ivy,
now both are full well grown,
Of all the trees that are in the wood,
the holly bears the crown.

*Oh, the rising of the sun
and the running of the deer,
The playing of the merry organ,
sweet singing in the choir.*

The holly bears a blossom
as white as lily flower,
And Mary bore sweet Jesus Christ
to be our sweet saviour

The holly bears a berry
as red as any blood,
And Mary bore sweet Jesus Christ
to do poor sinners good.

The holly bears a prickle
as sharp as any thorn,
And Mary bore sweet Jesus Christ
on Christmas Day in the morn.

The holly bears a bark
as bitter as any gall,
And Mary bore sweet Jesus Christ
for to redeem us all.

O Mother Blest

Composed by St Alphonsus Liguori, (1696-1787), and translated by E. Vaughan

O Mother blest, whom God bestows
On sinners and on just,
What joy, what hope thou givest those
Who in thy mercy trust.

Thou art clement, thou art chaste,
Mary, thou art fair;
Of all mothers sweetest, best,
None with thee compare.

O heavenly Mother, mistress sweet!
It never yet was told
That suppliant sinner left thy feet
Unpitied, unconsoled.

O Mother, pitiful and mild,
Ccase not to pray for me;

For I do love thee as a child,
And sigh for love of thee.

Most powerful Mother, all men know
Thy Son denies thee nought;
Thou askest, wishest it, and lo!
His power thy will hath wrought.

O Mother blest, for me obtain,
Ungrateful though I be,
To love that God who first could deign
To show such love for me.

Hail, Queen of heaven

Composed by Fr John Lingard, (1771-1851), a priest and historian who wrote extensively on the Reformation's disastrous effect on English cultural and religious life. His work was influential on William Cobbett's on History of the Protestant Reformation.

Hail, Queen of heaven, the ocean star,
Guide of the wanderer here below,
Thrown on life's surge, we claim thy care,
Save us from peril and from woe.

Mother of Christ, Star of the sea
Pray for the wanderer, pray for me.

O gentle, chaste, and spotless Maid,
We sinners make our prayers through thee;

Remind thy Son that He has paid
The price of our iniquity.

Virgin most pure, Star of the sea,
Pray for the sinner, pray for me.

And while to Him Who reigns above
In Godhead one, in Persons three,
The Source of life, of grace, of love,
Homage we pay on bended knee:

Do thou, bright Queen, Star of the sea,
Pray for thy children, pray for me.

Sleep! Holy Babe!

Composed by Edward Caswall

Sleep! Holy Babe! upon Thy mother's breast;
Great Lord of earth and sea and sky,
How sweet it is to see Thee lie
In such a place of rest,
In such a place of rest.

Sleep! Holy Babe! Thine angels watch around,
All bending low with folded wings,
Before th'incarnate King of kings,
In reverent awe profound.
In reverent awe profound.

Sleep! Holy Babe! while I with Mary gaze
In joy upon that face awhile,

Upon the loving infant smile
Which there divinely plays.
Which there divinely plays.

Sleep! Holy Babe! ah! take Thy brief repose;
Too quickly will Thy slumbers break,
And Thou to lengthened pains awake
That death alone shall close,
That death alone shall close.

In the bleak mid-winter

Composed by Christina Rossetti, (1830-1894)

In the bleak mid-winter
Frosty wind made moan,
Earth stood hard as iron,
Water like a stone;
Snow had fallen, snow on snow,
Snow on snow,
In the bleak mid-winter
Long ago.

Our God, Heaven cannot hold Him
Nor earth sustain;
Heaven and earth shall flee away
When He comes to reign:
In the bleak mid-winter
A stable-place sufficed
The Lord God Almighty,
Jesus Christ.

Enough for Him, whom cherubim
Worship night and day,
A breastful of milk
And a mangerful of hay;
Enough for Him, whom angels
Fall down before,
The ox and ass and camel
Which adore.

Angels and archangels
May have gathered there,
Cherubim and seraphim
Thronged the air,
But only His mother
In her maiden bliss,
Worshipped the Beloved
With a kiss.

What can I give Him,
Poor as I am?
If I were a shepherd
I would bring a lamb,
If I were a wise man
I would do my part,
Yet what I can I give Him,
Give my heart.

The angel Gabriel

Translated by Sabine Baring-Gould (1834-1924), from a Basque carol

The angel Gabriel from heaven came,
his wings as drifted snow, his eyes as flame;
"All hail," said he, "thou lowly maiden Mary,
most highly favoured lady," Gloria!

"For know a blessed Mother thou shalt be,
all generations laud and honour thee,
thy Son shall be Emmanuel, by seers foretold,
most highly favoured lady," Gloria!

Then gentle Mary meekly bowed her head,
"To me be as it pleaseth God," she said,
"my soul shall laud and magnify his holy Name."
Most highly favoured lady, Gloria!

Of her, Emmanuel, the Christ, was born
in Bethlehem, all on a Christmas morn,
and Christian folk throughout the world will ever say-
"Most highly favoured lady," Gloria!

MARY IN THE BIBLE

The following Biblical passages relate to Our Lady. Those from the Old Testament indicate that Mary can be seen as being prefigured, in the prophetic sense, as the mother of the Redeemer and Messiah, while those from the New Testament show how her life with Christ unfolded.

OLD TESTAMENT PASSAGES

Genesis 3:9-15 – the *Protoevangelium* – the Promise of the Redeemer

After the Fall of Adam and Eve, God punished the devil and promised that the offspring of the woman, Jesus, the New Adam, son of Mary, the New Eve, would crush the head of Satan. This is the *Protoevangelium,* the "first Gospel," the promise of the Redeemer to come in the fullness of time.

Genesis 28:12-15 – Jacob's Ladder as a type of Mary

Just as Jacob saw in a vision a ladder extending from earth to heaven, so is Mary the ladder by which Jesus descended to earth, taking on human nature, as well as being the way, as the Mediatrix of all graces, by which through her intercession we receive grace.

Exodus 3:1-4 – The Burning Bush as a type of Mary

Just as Moses saw the bush burning, but it was not consumed, so Mary's virginity remained whole before, during and after Christ's birth, as she became a mother in a miraculous way.

Exodus 40:20 – the Ark of the Covenant as a type of Mary

Just as the Ark contained the tablets of the Mosaic Law, so Mary bore the heir to this Law, Jesus Christ, and just as the Ark was covered inside and out with gold, so Mary, the new Ark of the Covenant, shone with the golden brilliance of a matchless purity.

Numbers 17 – Aaron's rod as a type of Mary

Just as Aaron's rod sprouted miraculously, giving forth buds, blossoms and fruit, so Mary brought forth Christ without loss of her virginity and free from pain, as the temple of the Holy Spirit.

Judges 6:36-40 – Gideon's Fleece as a type of Mary

Just as Gideon's fleece was wet while the ground was dry around it on the first morning, while it was dry and the ground wet the next day, so firstly the Son of God descended from heaven into her womb, and secondly, Mary was full of grace from her conception while the rest of humanity was affected by original sin.

Isaiah 7:14-16 – the prophetic sign of the Virgin Birth

Isaiah gave King Ahaz the sign of the Virgin Birth of the Son who would be called Emmanuel, that is, "God with us," in other words the Incarnation of Christ at Bethlehem, through the miracle of the Virgin Birth.

Ezekiel 44:2 – Mary as the Eastern Gate of the Temple

Just as the Eastern Gate of the Temple, according to Ezekiel, would remain shut because the Lord, the God of Israel, had passed through it, so Mary was the closed Gate who retained her virginity after the birth of Christ.

Micah 5:2-3 – the Ruler of Israel, the Messiah, is to come from Bethlehem

Jesus was born in Bethlehem to Mary, as the prophet Micah had foretold: his origin was from of old, from ancient days, because he was the incarnate Son of God.

NEW TESTAMENT PASSAGES

Luke 1:26-38 – the Annunciation of the Angel Gabriel to Mary, who told her that she was to be the Mother of God. Mary's yes to God led to the Incarnation of Jesus in her womb.

Luke 1:39-45 – this passage deals with the Visitation of Mary to her cousin Elizabeth, who was carrying St John the Baptist, and was the occasion of her hymn of praise, the Magnificat.

Matthew 1:18-24 – the Birth of Our Lord to Our Lady. St Matthew's account focuses on how an Angel of the Lord appeared to St Joseph in a dream to reassure him that Mary had remained faithful and that she had conceived her child by the power of the Holy Spirit.

Luke 2:1-14 – the Birth of Our Lord; after Mary and Joseph had gone to Bethlehem for Caesar Augustus's census, Jesus was born there in humility and poverty, because there was no place for them at the inn.

Luke 2:15-20 – the Shepherds go to see the Holy Family; after they had been told of Christ's birth by a vision of angels, the shepherds visited the Holy Family in their shelter at Bethlehem.

Luke 2:22-40 – the Presentation of the Child Jesus in the Temple forty days after his birth by Mary and Joseph. When the aged Simeon saw the Child, he foretold that a sword of sorrow would pierce the Blessed Virgin's heart at the time of the crucifixion.

Matthew 2:1-12 – the Visit of the Wise Men to see the Child Jesus. After King Herod had tried to deceive the Magi they visited the Holy Family at Bethlehem, but returned by a different way to their own country . This is the Epiphany, or manifestation of Christ to the Gentiles.

Luke 2:41-51 – the finding of the Child Jesus in the Temple by Mary and Joseph. After he had been missing for three days, his parents found him, but did not understand when he told them that he had been about his Father's affairs.

John 2:1-11 - The Wedding Feast at Cana saw the public manifestation of Jesus as the Messiah, as he turned the water into wine for the guests at the behest of his mother, Mary, thus anticipating his "hour" when his mission as the Redeemer of all mankind would begin.

John 19:25-27 – this passage describes Mary at the foot of the Cross of her Son, Jesus. He gave John to her as her son, and confided John to Mary as his mother, an indication of how all Christians, who are brothers of Christ, are also Mary's spiritual children.

Acts of the Apostles 1:12-14; 2:1-4 – Mary, as the Spouse of the Holy Spirit was at the descent of the same Holy Spirit at Pentecost, when the disciples were filled with his power and were able to boldly proclaim the Faith.

Revelation 11:19; 12:1-6,10 – Mary is the Woman of the Apocalypse, the new ark of the covenant, now assumed into heaven, the Woman clothed with the sun, who also has the moon under her feet, symbols of her power as Mother and intercessor for all mankind.

REFERENCES

St Aldhelm's *In basilica beatæ Mariæ semper virginis*, from Clayton, *The Cult of the Virgin Mary in Anglo-Saxon England*, p.91.

St Bede's *In natali sanctæ Dei genitricis* from Clayton, *The Cult of the Virgin Mary in Anglo-Saxon England*, p.93.

Book of Nunnaminster prayer from Clayton, *The Cult of the Virgin Mary in Anglo-Saxon England*, p.98.

Book of Cerne prayer from Clayton, *The Cult of the Virgin Mary in Anglo-Saxon England*, p.99.

Winchcombe Psalter prayer from Clayton, *The Cult of the Virgin Mary in Anglo-Saxon England*, p.109.

Aelfwine Winchester prayer and Litany from Clayton, *The Cult of the Virgin Mary in Anglo-Saxon England*, pp.110-11.

Oratio ad dei Genitricem from Clayton, *The Cult of the Virgin Mary in Anglo-Saxon England*, p.111.

Thomas of Elmham's *Te Deum Mariale* in Attwater, *A Dictionary of Mary*, p.283.

Post-Reformation Prayer to Our Lady in Attwater, *A Dictionary of Mary*, p.71.

Cardinal Newman prayer to Our Lady from *My Favorite Prayers and Novenas*, ML Trouve, Boston, 1997.

Pope John XXIII Marian prayer from *A Marian Prayer Book : A Treasury of Prayers, Hymns, and Meditations*, ed. Pamela Moran, Servant Publications, 1991, p.228.

Pope Paul VI Prayer to Mary from *A Marian Prayer Book: A Treasury of Prayers, Hymns, and Meditations*, Moran, p.228.

Pope John Paul II Prayer to Mary, Mother of the Church from *A Marian Prayer Book: A Treasury of Prayers, Hymns, and Meditations*, Moran, 1991.